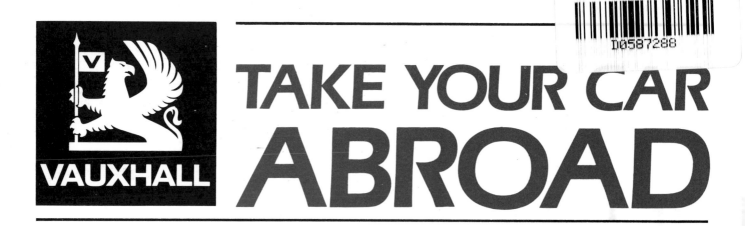

VAUXHALL

TAKE YOUR CAR ABROAD

GORDON COLE

LONDON

IAN ALLAN LTD

Acknowledgements

First published 1987

ISBN 0 7110 1755 7

Published by Ian Allan Ltd, Shepperton, Surrey; and printed by Ian Allan Printing Ltd at their works at Coombelands in Runnymede, England

I thank my friends most sincerely for the time and patience necessary to arrange the photographs. I thank the following Embassies for their assistance and co-operation which they willingly gave me.

Austrian
Belgian
Danish
Finnish
French
German (Federal Republic)
Italian
Luxembourg
Dutch
Norwegian
Portuguese
Spanish
Swedish
Swiss

References and extracts are from: 'Roadcraft' (material is reproduced with the permission of the Controller of Her Majesty's Stationery Office). Accident statistics supplied by RoSPA. All photography was by the author using Leica R4 and R5 cameras and Leica lenses from 35mm Summilux Rf/1.4 50mm Summilux Rf/1.4 and 135mm Elmarit Rf/2.8 focal lengths. Developing and printing by Kingsley Michael, Letchworth, Hertfordshire (Tel: 04626-79427). A special thank you to Vauxhall Motors Ltd, Luton, who so kindly supplied the vehicles. Ski lock and skis from Countryside Camping Ltd, High Street, Stevenage. Ian Allan Travel Ltd, who organised my travel arrangements. Most of all, however, I'd like to thank those members of the general public in Europe who — unwittingly — helped make the content in the photographs more realistic for me.

Gordon Cole

By producing this highly illustrated book on driving in Europe, the author and Vauxhall Motors Ltd seek to make a major contribution towards road safety, furthering the aims of European Road Safety Year 1986 in 12 countries.

Each year General Motors invests millions of pounds on research and development in new products, much of it devoted to vehicle safety.

The Vauxhall range of models — the most comprehensive on offer from any manufacturer in the UK — has won a series of distinguished awards.

In 1985 the Vauxhall Astra was named European Car of the Year and in 1987 the new Vauxhall Carlton also won this coveted accolade. In making this award, a panel of judges, consisting of 57 of the most prominent Motoring Journalists of 17 European countries, consider contenders from all manufacturers.

The prestigious Fleet Car of the Year Award for the car chosen by major fleet operators as the best value for money, has been won by the Vauxhall Cavalier in each of the three years (1985, 1986 and 1987) that it has been offered.

In 1986 Vauxhall received the Company Car Award for the manufacturer offering the best product range and service to fleet operators. 36,000 fleet operators completed a ques-tionnaire sponsored by *Company Car* magazine and the fleet management company, PHH Ltd.

In 1985 the Vauxhall Cavalier was named Holiday Car of the Year in a Pleasurewood Holidays/*Motor* magazine poll of holiday motorists.

Contents

Right:
Holidaymakers disembark from Townsend Thoresen's *Viking Voyager* at the French port of Cherbourg. From this point onwards a driver must think 'Right'. *J. R. Falconer*

Introduction

There is a lot to be gained from a driving holiday in Europe — the landscape, the architecture, the food, the people and the customs are so much closer to the driver, so much more tangible than the pleasures experienced on a package holiday. But, unfortunately, many people who would like to enjoy the experience of driving through Europe are put off by the superficial problems — the language, the road signs or, that most foreign thing of all, driving on the right. So they end up flying over the places that would be of most interest.

Take Your Car Abroad is not a travel guide to tempt you into this sort of holiday, but a book that should take away the fear of the unknown and, it is hoped, make more accessible the highways and byways of Europe. It explains some of the idiosyncrasies of European traffic rules and signs; shows some of the things the reader could encounter while on holiday and the best way round the difficulties. Above all, it is intended to ensure that a motoring holiday is incident free.

Road Safety

1986 was European Road Safety Year in which 12 countries were involved; their aim was to publicise five objectives for improving road safety all over Europe. The five objectives are detailed below.

Speed

Speed is often looked upon as something dangerous in itself: it isn't. What is dangerous is the use of speed in the wrong place or at the wrong time. There are many factors that have contributed towards accidents that should never have occurred — lack of concentration or road observation, inexperience, driving a strange or defective vehicle, aggression, ill-health, adverse weather conditions, poor road surfaces. Any one of these factors combined with excessive speed can be the cause of an accident.

The onus is always on the driver to select a speed that is safe for the prevailing conditions. Thus the expert driver will drive at a speed that is governed at all times by the amount of road that can be seen to be clear and the prevailing conditions at the time. In doing so he will be able to stop the vehicle well within the distance required for the speed being travelled, be it day or night and in any type of weather.

The Fixed Penalty Scheme for traffic offences became law in the United Kingdom on 1 October 1986. Many countries in Europe have been operating the same scheme for some time, but there is one major difference. In Europe the legal process has been taken one stage further, whereby the penalty has to be paid at the time the offence is committed. In the UK one has 28 days to pay the penalty and if the fixed penalty is not paid within the 28 days, it will automatically be increased by 50% and the increased fixed penalty will be recovered by the court as a fine.

Drinking and Driving

Drinking and driving has been the cause of many accidents and has resulted in the serious injury or death of many innocent people. Statistics show that over one thousand people are killed each year in the United Kingdom, as the result of drinking and driving. Pain and suffering is inflicted on innocent people by thoughtless and selfish road users, driving all types of vehicle under the influence of alcohol. The unconcerned attitude of some road users for the safety of others should not be tolerated for any reason.

Some countries in Europe have more stringent drink/drive laws than the United Kingdom. So if you are thinking about attending a beer festival or similar event, you ought to remember that consuming alcohol at such a festive time is no excuse for breaking the law. The police are entitled to require a driver to take a breathalyser test; failure to comply will result in a forensic examination. Should the result of such an examination be positive, then the penalty is extremely severe in all countries — particularly in some. Prison sentences certainly don't make for a good holiday!

Seat Belts

There can be no doubt that many thousands of car drivers and passengers all over Europe owe their lives to seat belts. The number of vehicle occupants killed or injured has decreased substantially since wearing seat belts became law in most countries. In some, a passenger occupying a rear seat must wear a seat belt if it is fitted.

When a car crashes, it stops very suddenly, unlike the driver and any passengers who will go on moving forward until they hit something — the windscreen, dashboard or some other part of the interior of the vehicle. It is this *second* collision that is the cause of injury or death.

No one can foresee the unexpected: it is better to take every safety precaution possible to reduce the risk of injury, pain, suffering or damage to passengers, drivers and their vehicles. In short, wear your seat belt!

Pedestrians

Statistics show that children under six years old and adults over the age of 65 constitute a high risk category in road accidents. When young children play they forget everything, including road traffic. They have no sense of danger; their game or toy is all that matters to them, therefore their movements are very unpredictable.

If you are not concentrating or if you are driving too fast for the prevailing conditions you will in all probability be unable to prevent an accident, if someone steps out into the road. It isn't just children who are at risk, the elderly have difficulty in estimating the distance and speed of approaching vehicles, their physical and mental powers may have declined and their ability to think and act is slower than that of a younger person. Failing eyesight can be assisted by spectacles, hearing by a hearing aid, but drivers should not assume that they have been seen or heard. The elderly will in all probability not cross the road at the

Above left:
There's no doubt what is being indicated here. The traffic sign, combined with the figures of children painted on the road, shows potential danger. Appropriate action should be taken (mirror, signal, speed) so that the driver will be ready to slow down or stop as required.
All photographs taken by the author

Left:
When passing a row of stationary vehicles, there's always a possibility that pedestrians will step out from between them. Where such dangers exist it is safer if you can adopt a position nearer the crown of the road to obtain a better view. This will give the driver more space in which to take avoiding action, should it become necessary.

ROAD SAFETY

Right:
In most countries in Europe trams and trolleybuses are the main forms of public transport in large cities. At some stages passengers alight on to the pavement or purpose-built islands, as here. The pedestrians have just got off the tram and speed should be reduced, bearing in mind that some pedestrians will cross the road without looking.
Location: Antwerp, Belgium

correct place of crossing; lack of judgement and anticipation has been a major contributory factor to the cause of many fatal accidents, and you should take nothing for granted. In every country you visit or pass through, there will be pedestrians of all ages crossing the road. It is all too easy to lose concentration looking at the scenery. You must be aware of pedestrians. Look out for them and anticipate their movements: in doing so you can prevent an accident.

Two-Wheeled Road Users

Two-wheeled road users — motorcyclists, cyclists, scooter or moped users — are at considerable risk on the roads today. Two-wheeled road users are more vulnerable to injury. Numerous countries have their own laws and attitudes regarding riders of mopeds; one difference, for example, is age. In one country a person at the age of 14 can ride a moped and no licence is required; in another country the minimum age is 16 and a driving licence is required. A safety helmet is a legal requirement in one country and not in another. Training in roadcraft and machine control is a statutory requirement in one country, and in another it is a more casual arrangement due to lack of facilities. Wherever one travels, it should always be borne in mind that roads have not been built for the exclusive use of drivers of motorcars, but for all who have the privilege and legal requirements needed to use them. In doing so one should not forget the pedestrians who have to cross the roads, at any time and in all types of weather; their safety depends on you, the driver.

Above left:
The young moped riders in Basel, Switzerland, do not have to wear safety helmets — but a helmet must be worn if a machine has an engine of 50cc or over.

Far left:
As the traffic sign shows, this dual carriageway en route from Belgium to Holland, has a purpose-built cyclepath for cyclists, mopeds and other slow-moving vehicles that are restricted from using the dual carriageway.

Left:
The confused pedestrian using the designated crossing in a town in Holland is being confronted by two cyclists. It would appear that one of the cyclists is also confused as to the direction of travel that should be taken.

ROAD SAFETY

1 Travelling to Europe

Travelling to the continent has never been as easy or comfortable as it is today. Improvements in travel agencies, tour operators and holiday companies have all played their part, as has the considerable improvement in car ferries. In the summer of 1928, a Capt Stuart Townsend, an army officer, chartered a collier called the *Artificer* and converted her to carry 15 cars and 12 drivers. Capt Townsend had taken his car to France in 1926 on a Southern Railway's ship, but in transit the car was damaged and the journey proved expensive. He was determined to prove that this sort of crossing could be economical yet profitable. In 1930 he bought a disused minesweeper, the *Forde*, converted her for car ferry work, and in that year she carried 5,000 cars and 12,000 people between Dover and Calais.

A ramp was first used on the *Forde* in 1936 so that cars could be driven on and off the ferry; this could only be achieved when tidal conditions allowed, otherwise they had to be lifted on board. The fare in 1936 from Dover to Calais was from £2 for cars and from 12s (60p) for passengers — a far cry from today's prices and vessels! The most recent ferries in use today can each carry up to 1,300 passengers and 350 cars and have a service speed of 22kt. A company that has three ships in service at the same time with identical carrying capacity, making between them up to 30 crossings a day would give a total capacity of 40,000 passengers and 10,000 cars each day. On the Dover-Calais route, ferries make the crossing in a scheduled 75min, although record crossings have been made in just over 50min. Features of the new ferries include restaurants, duty-free supermarkets, perfume and gift shops and a *bureau de change*. The last of these is not always available, so it is important that you carry adequate foreign currency for your immediate needs on arrival. There are elevators and service lifts available for elderly and disabled passengers that will take them from the car deck to the passenger deck.

There is now a very wide choice of ferry routes to the continent, and the chosen route will obviously depend on the final destination — although if you arrive too late you may be lucky just to get across the Channel. The motorway systems in both Britain and Europe will help you reach your destination quickly. You can get a good idea of the ports on both sides of the Channel and plan the best destination for your holiday by going to the local travel agent, who will be pleased to assist you in making your travel arrangements. The shortest sea crossing is from Dover to Calais — but, naturally, it is also the most heavily used of any of the sea routes to the continent. Ferries carry a large proportion of the 12 million people who went through the port in 1981. Since the 1950s there has been a dramatic increase in all kinds of traffic using the port, particularly passengers and accompanied motor vehicles. The increasing use of roll-on roll-off freight facilities now enables approximately half a million lorries to use Dover each year.

Ferries today have a drive on/drive off facility, which has been achieved by using clam-shell loading doors at the bow and stern ends, thus enabling vehicles to be driven on at one end and off at the other. It was in 1965 that the first drive through ferry was introduced and was used on the shortest Channel crossing. The modern ferry is a complex organisation, using various decks to accommodate freight, cars and passengers in comfort and as efficiently as possible in the space available.

Booking Your Ferry

Today the only problems involved in booking your ferry are the number of people travelling at peak times . . . and paying for the ticket! Choosing the right route and making the booking can be handled easily by your local travel agent or through a motoring organisation like the AA. Once you have booked your crossing, the travel agency will confirm the place through its computerised booking system. What could be easier?

Preparing the Vehicle

It is remarkable just how many drivers take a vehicle abroad without any preparation for the journey and then seem surprised when a mechanical failure occurs and their holiday is ruined. Always make sure that your vehicle has been well serviced before your holiday. Even after a major service you are advised to check all fluid levels and tyre pressures the day before you intend to travel. A tip on tyre pressures: it is very important that you check all the tyres when they are cold and keep to the tyre manufacturers' recommended pressures — bear in mind the weight the vehicle will have to carry, the number of passengers and luggage. Incorrect tyre pressures can be the cause of many problems and could result in an accident.

Lights

The lights on a right-hand drive car are set in a different way to those used on the continent. It is essential that an adjustment is made to the headlamps so that the beams do not light the wrong side of the road and dazzle approaching traffic. Alternatively headlamp converters (PVC mask sheet) or beam deflectors (clip-on lenses) could be used. However, beam deflectors must not be used with quartz halogen lamps. Headlamps with the beam dipped should be used in conditions of fog, snowfall, heavy rain and when entering a tunnel. The flashing of headlights should be avoided unless it is used as a warning of your approach, or at night as a warning to the driver in front that you are about to overtake.

In Sweden, the use of dipped headlights during the day is compulsory; the same applies to Finland but only outside built-up areas. In France and Tunisia, vehicles that are locally registered are equipped with headlights that show a yellow beam. To achieve a yellow beam, you could paint the lenses with a yellow plastic paint; this combined with headlamp converters will comply with the law. It should not be forgotten that on the return to the United Kingdom the converters or deflectors must be removed before the vehicle is driven on the highway; plastic paint can be removed with a solvent.

Below left:

It is of the utmost importance that you check tyre pressures and the condition of the tyres. Any defect found should be rectified before you start your journey.

Below:

Self-adhesive headlamp converters in place on the headlamp lenses. On a vehicle that has a four-headlamp system, only the dip-beam outer headlamps have to be converted. Full fitting instructions are supplied with headlamp converter kits.

D043 LNM

1 TRAVELLING TO EUROPE

The Law

Any vehicle that is going to be used on the continent must carry certain items of safety equipment — indeed you are required by law in many countries to do so. If you do not you will be breaking the law, and at the same time put your safety and that of your passengers at risk. The owner of any vehicle which is going to be driven in a foreign country should acquaint himself before departure with the local requirements. Information on this is obtainable through the AA. All the safety equipment and accessories mentioned in this section can be hired from your nearest Vauxhall/Opel dealer or from the Automobile Association. The cost involved for hiring the necessary equipment is nominal — and often part-refundable depending on use — and certainly cheaper than paying for it on the spot.

The United Kingdom has many laws relating to traffic and its use on the public highway — for example, the Road Traffic Act, the Motor Vehicles (Driving Licences) Regulations, and Construction and Use Regulations. These Acts and Regulations are amended from time to time and it is very difficult to keep an up-to-date record of them. When one includes all the Traffic Acts/Regulations appertaining to all the countries in Europe as well, the task is well-nigh impossible. The information given in this book concentrates on the most obvious points and was correct at the time of going to press. Most European road traffic laws are similar to those of the United Kingdom. Comparing the UK's Highway Code to that of another European country shows that some things differ slightly but the objective is the same. So while common sense should be enough most of the time, it is certainly worthwhile to check on the laws of the country you are going to — and also its traffic signs. While the international traffic signs are fairly standard, much of the wording on traffic signs is less easy to comprehend.

Right:
Traffic laws are very similar across Europe; these two signs from Portugal speak for themselves.

Safety Equipment and Accessories

There is a large variety of equipment and accessories which can be carried either to help in an emergency or simply to make the journey easier. The accompanying photographs illustrate many of them. The most useful are detailed below.

Nationality plate: This is self-adhesive and should be placed on the rear of your vehicle (and caravan or trailer). Motoring organisations and ferry companies usually supply it free of charge. Its use is compulsory and it is an offence in Europe to fail to display a nationality plate or to display an incorrect one. The approved sign is a white oval with black lettering and sized at least 6.9in by 4.5in.

Warning triangle: There are two types of warning triangle (see accompanying photograph). The triangle is folded and stored in its own plastic container.

Warning lamp: A warning lamp with an amber-coloured lens is not compulsory, but it is a useful piece of equipment to warn approaching traffic of a disabled vehicle in the hours of darkness, heavy rain, on the approach to a bend, in a tunnel and dead ground.

Fire extinguisher: There are two types available for use in emergencies — a dry powder extinguisher for simple fires or a halon version for engine and electrical fires.

Spare bulb kit: A set of replacement bulbs will help you avoid unnecessary inconvenience when garages are closed.

First aid kit: The first aid kit contains everything you are likely to need in dealing with minor accidents, and mishaps.

Tow rope: This is recommended, as problems can occur at any time and a tow rope could assist you or some other road user.

Headlamp converter: This is a compulsory requirement if headlamps have not been adjusted (see above).

Snow chains: These are compulsory in some countries during winter.

Left:
This is the minimum selection of safety equipment and accessories that should be taken. They should be stored in the luggage compartment and be readily available.

1 TRAVELLING TO EUROPE

Spiked tyres: These are allowed to be used in some countries under certain conditions, ie in deep snow or ice. But not to be used when the road has been salted, thus the spikes would damage the road surface.

Base and luggage carrier: The luggage carrier is attached to the base carrier. It is ideal for carrying that extra piece of luggage that will not fit into the boot. But it must be borne in mind that all heavy luggage should not be carried on the roof, otherwise the stability of the vehicle will be affected which is potentially dangerous.

Ski carrier lock: When going on a skiing holiday, there is only one way of transporting skis safely, and that is by using a carrier specially designed for the job. A ski lock is compulsory in some countries. Not only will it secure the safety of the skis while in transit, but that of other luggage as well. It is important that the skis are loaded on to the vehicle correctly — with the back end of the skis at the front and the tips of the skis facing the rear. By loading skis in this way they will not get damaged in transit and at the same time will not affect the stability of the vehicle or cause distraction to the driver flapping about. To complete the safe transportation of skis, a cover should be placed over the bindings. This will have the added benefit of preventing dirt, salt etc entering the bindings. The poles should be carried inside the vehicle, otherwise the straps will flap about in the wind if they are carried in the ski lock.

Above right:

A base and luggage carrier. Note the security locks on the base carrier. The base carrier is the foundation for other types of carriers, ie sailboard, bicycle, boat and skis.

Right:

The Vauxhall/Opel approved base carrier is mounted and secured to the roof rails. The ski locks fit on to each of the base carriers and are secured by clamps. Note the anti-theft locks on the base carrier and on the ski locks.

Far right, top:

With the skis in position on the block, the top bar is brought down and clamps the skis in the block. The ski lock is designed to take three pairs beside each other.

Far right, bottom:

Ready to go!

Driving Mirrors

When you leave the port — if you haven't done so already — you are advised to pull up somewhere safe and adjust the interior and exterior mirrors for maximum rear view observation. You must always remember that the immediate danger will be on your left when you are being overtaken, when you are about to overtake and when you are about to turn left. You must have properly adjusted mirrors and you must use them. A good driver is aware of the situation behind him as well as to the front. This can only be achieved by self-discipline and practice. And when you look in the mirrors, you must pay attention to what you see and make effective use of what they show well before signalling, changing direction, slowing down or stopping. An offside mirror (nearside in the UK) is a legal requirement in many countries in Europe. For the visitor it is an essential safety factor — without it a driver will not know if it is safe to change course and rear view observation will be inadequate. Make sure you have the appropriate mirrors fitted to the vehicle you intend to use in Europe.

Below:
With mirrors that are properly adjusted, a driver will be aware of the situation behind and beside him, as can be seen by this example.

1 TRAVELLING TO EUROPE

Documentation

There are certain documents that must go with you when you leave the country. You must ensure that they are valid and up-to-date on leaving the United Kingdom and when you return, otherwise numerous problems could arise.

Passport/Visa: Each person travelling outside the British Isles must have or be named on a passport. A visa is not normally required for Western European countries when visiting for periods of three months or less. However, if you hold a passport of any other nationality, a UK passport not issued in the United Kingdom, or are in any doubt at all about your position, you should check with the embassies or consulates of the countries you intend to visit.

Driving licence: You must take your national driving licence (not provisional) with you when driving abroad. The minimum age a person can drive in many countries is 18, therefore if a 17-year-old intends to drive they should check with the tourist office of the country in question.

International Driving Permit: The International Driving Permit is an internationally recognised document, issued by the Automobile Association for a statutory fee to persons 18 or over, holding a valid full (not provisional) United Kingdom driving licence. The International Driving Permit is compulsory in many countries in Europe, so you are advised to get one before you depart. Application forms for an IDP can be obtained from any Automobile Association travel agency or centre. When applying for an IDP you must produce your driving licence and a passport size photograph. The licence is valid for one year from the date of issue and cannot be renewed — you have to put in a new application each time.

Vehicle registration document: You must take the original vehicle registration document with you. If the vehicle is not registered in the driver's name, a letter of authority from the owner stating that a named person(s) is allowed to drive and use the vehicle in the country or countries stated. The letter of authority and vehicle registration document must be readily available should they need to be seen.

Road tax: Should the vehicle excise licence (road tax) expire while the vehicle is abroad, when it returns to the United Kingdom the driver/owner will commit an offence as soon as the public highway is used. You should therefore ensure that your road tax will not expire while you are away on holiday.

Insurance

Vehicle Insurance: As in the United Kingdom, motor vehicle insurance is compulsory in all European countries, but the degree of cover you have abroad depends on your policy. It is, therefore, a good idea to contact your insurance company to discuss your requirements and to get additional cover if required — if you intend to take a boat (with or without an engine) trailer, or caravan, you need to include it on your insurance. Should other drivers be covered? It need not be overstated just how important it is to have the right cover before you go abroad.

Carte Internationale D'Assurance Automobile (green card): Insurance policies issued in the United Kingdom and the Republic of Ireland automatically provide minimum cover in all EEC countries and additionally, certain countries which are not members — like Austria, Czechoslovakia, East Germany, Finland, Hungary, Norway, Sweden and Switzerland. Once you have decided how much insurance cover is required, your insurer/agent will issue an International Motor Insurance Card (green card). This is issued under the authority of the Motor Insurers Bureau and provides evidence that you have complied with the minimum insurance requirements for the country you intend to visit. You are advised to carry the green card with you, as it proves in an effective way that you have insurance cover.

Bail Bond: An accident in Spain can have serious consequences including impounding your car and property and the detention of the driver pending trial. It is therefore advisable to arrange a Bail Bond before you leave Britain. This is a written guarantee that a cash deposit of up to £1,500 will be paid to the Spanish Court as surety for bail and for any fine which may be imposed. A Bail Bond can be obtained from the insurer of your motor vehicle and it is certainly advisable to get one if Spain is included on your journey.

Breakdown Insurance: The Automobile Association offers a 5-Star Service policy that covers a variety of incidents that could ruin your holiday. Vehicle recovery, spare parts cover — it could make all the difference if you break down somewhere a long way from home.

Leaving the UK

It may seem like stating the obvious, but it is advisable to check that you have everything you need before you set out for the ferry port. Passports, travel tickets, insurance documents, visas — it is too late to remember something at the port or, worse still, be refused entry across the Channel.

Run through what you'll need well before you leave. A practice packing of your vehicle is also a good idea — remember that the weight should be evenly distributed and that you'll be in the car for some hours.

The following photographs show the typical sequence of events when you take a ferry abroad.

Far left:

When you arrive at the port entrance, you will enter a waiting area where traffic is marshalled into a ticket control, then on to passport and customs control. The passport and customs offices can be seen.

Above:

All passports are checked by a passport examiner, who can be seen waiting for the next travellers to produce their passports. Make sure you have yours!

Left:

After the passport(s) have been examined, you proceed to the waiting lanes of the appropriate ferry company with whom you are going to travel.

Right:
At some docks, there is a loading and departure schedule as shown here.

Far right, top:
There are some ferries that have double deck load and unload facility — as seen here.

Far right, bottom:
A marshal will request you to drive up/down a loading ramp, that will take you on to one of the vehicle decks, where you will be asked to park the vehicle. Ferry companies do expect rules regarding vehicles while on board to be complied with. (1) No petrol cans (full or empty) in the vehicles. (2) Switch off engine as soon as it is parked. (3) Apply the handbrake. (4) Select first or reverse gear before leaving vehicle. (5) Close all windows and lock all doors. (6) Vehicles powered by LPG should have tanks switched off. (7) No smoking on vehicle decks. (8) Make sure you have with you car keys and anything else you may need while on board.

Left:
The services on board a ferry are excellent, and a good selection of goods is available from the duty-free shops.

Above right:

This picture was taken on board a ferry about to dock. The bow door is being raised and the drive-off ramp can be clearly seen. When the ferry has docked, drivers will be marshalled off the ferry to a waiting area, then on to customs and passport examination. At this stage a driver must think 'Right', as from now on you'll be driving on the right-hand side of the road.

Right:

There are many traffic signs in Europe, but when leaving a port this is the first and last one to remind you on which side of the road you should be.

Reasons why entry into another country can be refused

When you leave Britain and arrive at the gateway to another country, you have no right of entry. Access can be refused for a variety of reasons — an out-of-date passport or driving licence or no proper international distinguishing sign (GB) on the back of the car. Obvious contravention of traffic laws could also constitute sufficient reasons for refusal of entry — for example a vehicle that has liquid propane gas either as a single or dual fuel system is banned in Portugal, and so cars using this system wouldn't be allowed in.

The important thing is to ensure that you have everything you need — up-to-date, valid and to hand — it is not difficult to do this, but it does require organisation. This checklist will help you remember everything you need either to leave the UK or enter another country.

Documents
Passport
Visa
Travel ticket
Driving licence
International Driving Permit
Vehicle registration document
Vehicle insurance
Green card (not compulsory, but advisable)
Bail bond (not compulsory, but advisable in Spain)
AA 5-Star cover (not compulsory! but advisable)

For the car
Headlight conversions
Nationality plate
Warning triangle
Snow chains (in winter)
Nearside mirror
Fire extinguisher
First aid kit
Spare bulb kit

Car phones

An increasing number of cars are fitted with telephones. These car phones are liable to confiscation by Continental customs officials because of the interference they cause to emergency radio frequencies on the Continent.

The equipment can be reclaimed from customs before the return ferry crossing. But better still, leave it at home.

2 Back to Basics

Are you a 'good' driver? When did you take your driving test? If you are going on a driving holiday in Europe, you will be on unfamiliar roads with wonderful distractions all round you. It is essential for your own safety and the safety of others that you drive competently.

This chapter runs through those basics that we all learnt when we took our driving test but which laziness or overfamiliarity has caused us to forget or corrupt. The publication *Advanced Driving* by Gordon Cole (Ian Allan Ltd, 1986) should also be consulted.

Driving Position

The driver should be in control of the vehicle at all times and the way you sit affects this. Don't slouch in the driving seat or sit too close to the steering wheel. Don't sit too far back, with the seat partially reclined and your arms fully extended. You may look like a motor racing champion but you aren't on a racetrack! The ideal seating position should allow you to operate the pedals without fuss and discomfort, and ensure that the hand controls and auxiliary switches are within easy reach. You should be sitting upright and alert, not taut or strained, yet not too relaxed. Steering characteristics vary from car to car. If you intend to drive an unfamiliar vehicle you may find that it will respond more (oversteer) or less (understeer) than you expect. You must quickly adapt yourself to the feel of the vehicle you are driving, so that you can control it properly in all conditions.

Both hands should remain on the wheel unless it is necessary to remove one or other to signal, operate an auxiliary switch, change gear, or perform another *driving* function. Any change from the straight course must be accomplished gradually and smoothly, other than when manoeuvring at slow speeds. The steering wheel should be turned by the 'pull and push' method. Most vehicles have steering which is self-straightening. You should not allow the steering wheel to spin back into place. This

Left:
This driver is in the ideal seating position that will assist him to maintain control of the vehicle, keep alert and reduce fatigue.

is lazy driving and potentially dangerous. Accordingly, the steering wheel should be fed back by hand movements, in the reverse order to which it was originally turned. If you are sitting properly, then you will control the car properly and safely.

Car Control

Of all the factors that contribute towards road accidents it is the presence of human beings — plain human error — that is the most important.

The driver of a right-hand vehicle in Europe has a great deal to think about — the conditions demand a high degree of concentration and observation. To help ensure road safety, everyone is taught as part of the driving test a form of the police system of car control devised by Lord Cottenham for the Metropolitan Police Driving School in 1937.

The system follows a standard sequence of events, each feature of which is considered by the driver at the approach to any hazard. It is the basis upon which the whole technique of good driving is built, and still forms the basis of instruction for police drivers today.

A hazard is anything which contains an element of actual or potential danger. There are three types:

(a) Physical features, such as a junction, roundabout, bend or dead ground (hill crest and steep dip).
(b) Those created by the position or movement of other road users.
(c) Those created by variations in road surface or weather conditions.

By definition, every feature of the system is considered at the approach to any hazard. Only those applicable to the particular circumstances are put into operation, but whichever features are selected, they must always be in the correct sequence. It is only by constant practice that skill in the application of the system can be acquired.

Features of the System

1 Course: Once you have seen a hazard you have to decide on the best line of approach. In essence this constitutes a driving plan for the particular hazard and later in this chapter we shall examine the sort of circumstances you need to anticipate. If this involves a change of your vehicle's position, look in the mirrors to see that it is safe to do so and make the necessary deviation signal.

2 Mirrors, Signal and Speed: Any reduction of speed for the hazard should be accomplished at this stage. But before changing speed you must check your mirrors again and consider whether a deviation signal is necessary to tell other road users of your intention to change course or slow down.
3 Gear: If you are changing speed then you should select the correct gear at this stage.
4 Mirrors and Signal: If a signal has not been necessary before the hazard, it might be necessary at the hazard — in which case, after checking in the mirrors, it should be given.
5 Horn: An audible warning may be necessary as well as a deviation signal.
6 Acceleration: A correct degree of acceleration is used to leave the hazard.

If you follow this drill at each hazard you come to, you will find that it becomes instinctive. However, one word of caution: in driving it is never a good idea to become fixed in your ideas. Because things can change so quickly you have to stay alert and flexible — so that you can change your driving plan as the circumstances warrant.

Observation

The use of mirrors has been stressed in the system of car control. Driving in Europe, on the 'wrong' side of the road, makes mirror work and all-round observation even more important if you are to drive well — especially such tricky manoeuvres as overtaking and turning left. Because of the blind area to your left rear the diligent use of mirrors — particularly the nearside one — is essential. If in doubt — or, indeed, simply as an additional check — you should look over your left shoulder before changing course or starting off.

But, of course, there are other factors in observation. To begin with you must keep your area of vision clear by keeping the windows and windscreen clean inside and out.

Stickers placed on the windscreen and other windows can obscure a driver's view, and should not be put there. In some vehicles, lucky charms and mascots can be seen hanging from the interior mirror; these swing about in front of the driver, distracting him and obscuring his view of the road, which is potentially dangerous. The mirrors should be properly adjusted so that the best possible view to the rear is gained.

The driver should make sure the windscreen wipers and washers are in good working order. Particles of dust and grit will at times collect on the windscreen, so the washers should be used to assist cleaning before the wipers are used, otherwise the windscreen could get scratched. Furthermore, the bodywork of the vehicle, ie roof supports, door pillars and other parts, can obstruct a driver's view. Adverse weather conditions too can greatly reduce effective observation.

Signals

Signals are the means by which drivers warn other road users of their intentions and presence. There are three types of visible signal fitted to every new car — the direction indicator signals, stop lamps and headlamps — and the driver's arm signal makes a fourth. They are the language of the road, and are the only visible way drivers can inform other road users and pedestrians of their intention and presence.

To be of any use, signals must be given clearly as illustrated in the Highway Code, and at the right time and place (Feature 2 in the system of car control). If no other road user or pedestrian is in sight then a signal is superfluous. However, it should be considered again at Feature 4 of the system.

A signal gives a warning, not an instruction, and gives you no right of way. Too many serious accidents are caused by drivers and motorcyclists who signal their intention to carry out a manoeuvre and then just do it without taking effective rear observation before changing course and regardless of the position and speed of other road users who could be following or overtaking them at the time.

Stop lamps: The stop lamps are fitted to the rear of the vehicle and are illuminated when the foot brake pedal is pressed. They provide a useful signal in circumstances where advance warning should be given of the intention to slow down or stop. It must be borne in mind that the stop lamps will not illuminate until the brakes are applied. Always look in the mirror before applying the foot brake.

Headlamps: The flashing of headlights should not be used for signalling in daylight unless in lieu of a horn warning for overtaking at speed on motorways, dual carriageways and other fast roads where an audible signal would prove inaudible because of the distance and speed. The length of the warning will be determined by circumstances, but in any case should consist only of one flash.

Arm signal: It would be impracticable under normal conditions for an arm signal to be given, if you are driving a right-hand drive vehicle in Europe, for obvious reasons.

Top left:
The driver is using the mirror before pulling away from the kerb. If no traffic is seen she will look over her left shoulder to make absolutely sure it is safe to move off.

Bottom left:
In some countries in Europe dust can be prominent, particularly in the summer; it is therefore advisable to have the car washed to remove the dust. In doing so, the driver and passenger(s) view will not be obstructed, at the same time making a contribution to a safe and pleasant holiday.

Above:

To be of any use, a signal must be given at the right time and place. This driver has signalled his intention to turn right in good time, by using a direction indicator signal.

Above right:

This Italian prohibitory sign warns a driver that use of an audible warning device is not allowed.

Right:

The pedestrian about to step off the footpath is not concentrating. A driver confronted with this situation should use the horn and reduce speed. *Location: Basel, Switzerland*

One signal many drivers do not use these days is an acknowledgement of a courtesy extended by another road user. All the driver should do to indicate appreciation is raise a hand; it should not be overdone, but neither should it be neglected, because its general use can do much to promote good road manners.

The horn: You should sound the horn only when it is really necessary. It is a *warning* of your presence, and — even though every other precaution has been taken — its use will at times be necessary to attract the attention of other road users, particularly pedestrians and cyclists unaware of your approach. You must remember that there are some areas where the use of an audible warning device is prohibited. If you are in one of those you should be particularly diligent. Your experience must determine whether a horn note is required. In heavy traffic its use should be rare, because speeds are moderate and other actions can be taken in good time. Once again though, you must remember that use of the horn gives no protection or right of way. There must have been fatal accidents caused by drivers using the horn and in so doing mistakenly assuming the road ahead will be clear by the time the hazard is reached. The horn warning should be used in good time, not in an aggressive manner or a way that will frighten other road users.

Far left, top:
Another Swiss pedestrian crossing the road at the wrong place.

Above left:
This Portuguese sign informs pedestrians to walk on the left-hand side of the road, therefore approaching traffic will be seen. Should a pedestrian(s) be walking on the right, appropriate action should be taken to ensure their safety.

Far left, bottom:
On the approach to a hazard on both sides of a main road — like this Portuguese market — every precaution should be taken by the driver. In doing so, pedestrians will be in no danger due to the presence of his vehicle.

Left:
These two ladies from a village in Portugal are walking on the wrong side of the road and are therefore unaware of the danger of approaching traffic.

2 BACK TO BASICS

Speed

Ever since the development of the motor vehicle, speed at the wrong time and place has been the cause of many accidents. The choice of speed must be related to the driver's concentration and ability, the type and limitation of the vehicle and the prevailing road traffic conditions. Remember that the safe speed for any given situation may change from second to second, and you must accelerate or decelerate to suit the circumstances. Speed is a relative factor which is often looked upon as being something dangerous in itself. It is not. What is dangerous is the wrong application of speed.

Driving Through Water

Driving at speed on surface water and in heavy rain can be dangerous, because waterlogged tyres will lead to 'aquaplaning' — more so if the tread depth of the front tyres is near the limit. Aquaplaning is a condition when the front tyres cannot cope with the surface water usually at speeds in excess of 50mph/80kph. When this happens, the tyres push superfluous water forward, creating a wedge; given time and distance, the tyres will mount the wedge and lose contact with the road. The symptoms of aquaplaning are light steering, and, if speed is maintained, complete loss of steering control. If you think you are aquaplaning, decelerate immediately, by reducing pressure from the accelerator but not by braking — even momentarily — because this will aggravate the condition. When speed has been reduced considerably the tyres will contact the road surface and steering control will be regained.

Driving at speed into unsuspected deep water — ie puddles or deep ruts — will in all probability wrench the steering wheel from the hands of the driver, as the wheel reaches the deepest point of the puddle or rut. In consequence, the driver will lose control. Flood water will collect quickly due to heavy rain or melting snow, especially in poorly drained low lying areas, or on uneven road surfaces, at the sides of a cambered road, and where there is a dip under a bridge or underpass. Many drivers disregard adverse weather conditions and drive too fast for the prevailing conditions. Maintaining an excessive speed in poor visibility caused by spray thrown up by heavy goods vehicles and/or the density of rain, will make flood water difficult to detect on any type of road; this creates a potential danger to the driver and other road users.

Top right:

The traffic sign warns a driver of the danger of a 'slippery road' with the risk of aquaplaning when the road surface is wet.

Bottom right:

Weather conditions can change dramatically, and in a short period of time, and it is not always feasible for warning signs to be placed in areas where danger to the road user is present. At night, the difference between a wet road surface and flood water is difficult to identify, and for some the consequence has put them and others in danger.

Speed Limits

National speed limits differ from one country to another, so you must be aware of the limits for the different areas and type of roads within that country. Ignorance of the facts is no excuse in law, should you be stopped by the police for exceeding the speed limit. On-the-spot fines for excessive speed can be very expensive.

Far left:

This traffic sign informs drivers entering Switzerland of the maximum speeds permitted in towns, the country and on motorways.

Left and below:

This sign in Spain not only informs a driver of the speed limits, but also warns of the minimum safe distance at the edge of the road. Imagine the problems if a driver did leave the road by one-and-a-half metres or more!

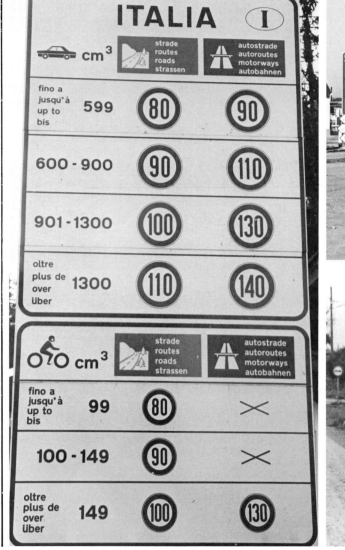

ITALIA Ⓘ

🚗 cm³	strade routes roads strassen	autostrade autoroutes motorways autobahnen
fino a jusqu'à up to bis 599	(80)	(90)
600 - 900	(90)	(110)
901 - 1300	(100)	(130)
oltre plus de over über 1300	(110)	(140)

🚲 cm³	strade routes roads strassen	autostrade autoroutes motorways autobahnen
fino a jusqu'à up to bis 99	(80)	✕
100 - 149	(90)	✕
oltre plus de over über 149	(100)	(130)

Right:
This sign on the border of Austria and Italy informs a driver of the speed limits and the road speeds for vehicles of the size of engine shown.

Far right, top:
A similar sign — different limits. This is in Portugal.

Far right, bottom:
Enforcement. The sign warns motorists that radar is used to check the speed of road users passing through the village. The maximum speed permitted on this Spanish road is 60kph.

Left:
This Spanish sign informs a driver that a crossing is coming up, where children and other danger could be present. It isn't visible from this location so you should immediately slow to 60kph and keep your eyes open.

Right:
This sign in Marbella, Spain, illuminates (as shown) when a vehicle approaches it at a speed greater than that of the permitted speed of 60kph and therefore warns a driver to reduce speed.

Far right:
The traffic sign painted on this road in Salzburg, Austria, reminds a driver that there is a 30kph speed limit.

Left:

A clear stretch of Spanish road. Take in its beauty at the legal speed limit. You'll lose time and money if you don't and you're caught!

Below left:

On the approach to a village or town the driver should prepare to lose speed, more so when descending a steep hill, as shown here in Spain.

Below:

This Spanish traffic sign informs a driver of a commercial vehicle that the speed limit is 60kph for a truck.

2 BACK TO BASICS

Above right:
The danger is obvious as is the warning that a 20kph speed limit is enforced on this Spanish hairpin bend.

Right:
The danger caused by the badly parked cars in this street in Portugal means that you would be advised to drive slowly.

Driving Plans

Although so much of driving is instinctive, nevertheless you should always have a driving plan — an awareness of what is going on around your vehicle and how you are going to deal with any hazards. Driving plans are based on three factors: what can be seen, what cannot be seen, and events which could reasonably be expected to happen.

What can be seen: Use of mirrors gives you an awareness of what is going on behind and to the side of you. Observation of the road ahead determines the course you must follow and, of course, your speed. Speed is determined by visibility — you must be able to stop in the distance that is seen to be clear. So your speed should be adjusted to suit the amount of road visible, or if the road conditions change and within the law.

What cannot be seen: If your visibility is restricted — by a bend or other obstruction — then you have to adjust your speed accordingly.

Things that could happen: No one can foresee the future and you can always be caught out by the unexpected. But certain things can reasonably be expected to happen — green traffic signals turn red; pedestrians waiting to cross a road could step out; a vehicle approaching from a side street could emerge. All these things and a host of others mean that continued vigilance is necessary. The accompanying photographs show some of the things that could happen.

Left:
What can be seen — a clear road, a traffic sign and well defined white lines on the road. You should be able to anticipate potential danger here without difficulty.

2 BACK TO BASICS

This page:
What can't be seen — four pictures that tell you what you can't see. Act on the information given by road signs and be on your guard.

Above left:
**Things that could happen —
this busy junction in
Strasbourg is full of potential
incident as the lights are
about to change.**

Far left:
**A driver who intends to turn
left over the bridge should
take full advantage of what
can and cannot be seen by
looking across the water.**

Left:
**It's hard to spot but there's a
crossroads after the bridge.
The junction should be
approached carefully.**

2 BACK TO BASICS

Above right:
Two pedestrians can be seen by a crossing, are they going to cross? Slow down, in case.

Far right, top:
A hazard — a horse and cart. But don't overtake until you can see whether the road ahead is clear — the road markings simply emphasise what is common sense.

Right:
An obvious hazard — reduction of speed is essential in order that you don't inconvenience or endanger the flock.

Far right, bottom:
Less obvious if you weren't concentrating. Is the dog obedient enough to wait for you to go past?

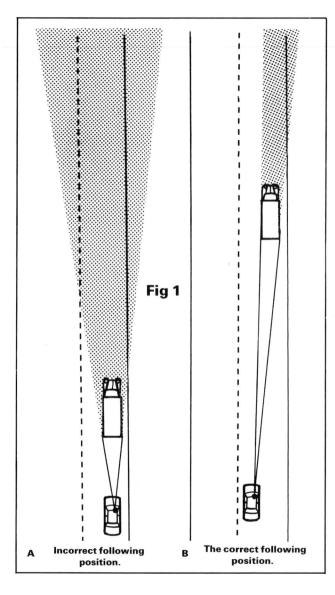

Fig 1

A   Incorrect following position.

B   The correct following position.

Positioning

An important part of any driving is the correct positioning of your vehicle in the roadway. You must be in the right place on the road at the approach to any hazard. You must take account of all the things you can and cannot see and of all the other factors mentioned in this chapter.

Naturally, this is easier in the UK for the driver of a right-hand drive vehicle than in Europe. The accompanying photographs give examples of the sort of obstacles you may encounter, but one particular example of road positioning needs to be stressed — the correct position to use when following another vehicle, particularly a large one.

Look at Figure 1a. The driver here is following the vehicle in front too closely. If you drive like this you won't be able to see any of the hazards ahead — which means that you'll have to react very quickly to a change of speed or direction by the vehicle in front. You can't make the decision to overtake because you can't see, and pulling out from this position would be dangerous. You can only increase your field of view marginally by lateral movement.

Now look at Figure 1b. By keeping back from the vehicle in front you have a good view of the road ahead which can be increased along the off or nearside by a very slight deviation. You can stop in time if the vehicle ahead stops quickly and give the vehicle behind you time enough to react as well. Finally you are perfectly placed to move up to overtake the vehicle ahead (see Chapter 4) when it is safe to do so.

2 BACK TO BASICS

Right:

The driver is in the correct position on the road. This enables him to obtain the best possible view of the road ahead and therefore increases his margin of safety. Note the caution sign on the right indicating ice on the carriageway.

Far right:

The driver approaching a railway bridge with the road narrowing on both sides, has assessed the situation in good time and positioned his car correctly. It is obvious that two cars cannot pass under the bridge at the same time, therefore the driver has taken the initiative and stopped his vehicle well before reaching the hazard. In so doing, has given the other driver precedence thus leaving nothing to chance. When the vehicle has passed and no other vehicle can be seen that can create a similar situation, the driver should look in the mirrors and consider the need for a direction indicator signal before moving off.

Right:

You should always be aware of the danger of approaching traffic. Keep an eye out for the 'lurker' — the car or motorcycle which closes right up behind a lorry and then swoops out into full view. A lurker can be seen here behind the approaching lorry. If it is safe to do so the driver should now position his vehicle further to the right until the danger has passed.

Left:
The start of a one-way system in Strasbourg. The sign on the right indicates junction ahead. Position the car carefully depending on which way you want to go.

Far left, bottom:
When parking is allowed in the middle of the road, a driver must always be aware of the possibility that a vehicle could move out into his path. In the distance a minibus can be seen parked in a space that is too short for the length of the vehicle and therefore it has protruded on to the carriageway.

On the approach to this hazard, a driver must use the mirrors and consider the use of a deviation signal before altering course. When it is safe to do so, a change of road position should be adopted so that the hazard can be passed with a good margin of safety.
Location: Reims, France

Left:
A driver passing a row of stationary vehicles on the right should look for potential danger; eg, a car door opening, a vehicle that could move out, or a pedestrian stepping out between the vehicles. It must be borne in mind that if a tram is present, it will be travelling in the same direction, therefore leaving little or no margin of safety should anything happen.

Right:

In some towns, bus lanes are marked with the word 'BUS' painted on the road, therefore should not be used by other vehicles. A No Stopping sign has also been painted on the road as a reminder to motorists. This is in Salzburg, Austria.

Far right:

Town driving in particular demands complete concentration. In places where traffic movement is slow, it becomes a matter of 'follow my leader'. The potential danger can be clearly seen in this one-way street in Antwerp. There are parked vehicles on the left, the cyclist could change course or stop at any moment. Note the kerbstones that separate the road from the tramway.

Right:

Patience is a virtue — particularly when driving. Here the temptation is to pull out to overtake the two cyclists. But this would mean driving on the track of a tramway. As the tramway alters course soon it may be best to wait — but if overtaking is essential, before positioning your vehicle in the right place, look in the mirrors. There could be a tram at your shoulder!
Location: Innsbruck, Austria

Far left:

A bus lane can be seen combined with road markings and a number of traffic signs. The triangular sign gives warning (vehicles approaching from the right), therefore you must expect vehicles from the right, although you have priority over them. The square sign with a white background indicates Direction of Priority road. The black broad line shows the direction of the main road, and drivers on the secondary roads must observe the 'Priority to the right' rule.
Location: Holland

Above left:

The refuge is a stopping-place for trams. A driver approaching a tram stop should be aware that when a tram is present, passengers could alight and cross the road without looking, and not be aware of the danger of approaching traffic. Note the Keep Right bollard that directs traffic away from the tramlines at this stage.
Location: Amsterdam, Holland

Left:

In Amsterdam, Holland, there are numerous narrow streets as this example shows. Some pedestrians prefer to walk in the narrow road instead of on the footpath that is provided between the poles. Note the No Waiting sign. Should a driver stop his vehicle in this one-way street, it would be blocked.

2 BACK TO BASICS

Right:
The road divides ahead. The sign in the distance means that the correct position on the road should be taken for the intended direction of travel. Note the two lanes sign going down the hill, thus helping you to position your vehicle in good time.

Far right, top:
The sign with white arrows informs a driver that a lane has been designated for vehicles intending to turn left ahead, combined with white diagonal stripes painted on the road to assist a driver to position his vehicle correctly for the intended manoeuvre.

Right:
This Belgian crossroads is very confusing, because while traffic lights control the movement of traffic, white arrows on the road indicate the direction of travel. When the green light is seen a driver should move off in the direction of the white arrow, but you should follow the direction of the second arrow and not the first, otherwise a potentially dangerous situation could occur. At times when the volume of traffic is heavy, the white lines will in all probability not be visible, thus being a contributory factor towards confusion.

3 | Junctions

Turning Left

Turning left at a crossroads is — after overtaking — possibly the most difficult and dangerous manoeuvre with which you will have to contend. It is particularly difficult because it is so easy to do so at home.

All you have to do is remember the basic system of car control when approaching a hazard (in this case the crossroads) and act accordingly in the stages outlined below and in Figure 2.

Course: Having decided that you must turn left at the crossroads, you must determine the best line of approach. Look in the mirrors and if it is necessary to signal do so, remembering to look again in the mirrors before manoeuvring.

Mirrors, Signals and Speed: The mirrors are again used, and if the intention is to turn left at the hazard, consideration must be given to a deviation signal. Any reduction in speed for the hazard will be accomplished at this stage, preceded by a slowing down signal if appropriate with the use of stop lamps.

Gear: The correct gear is selected for the speed of the vehicle following application of the second feature.

Mirrors and Signals: It is essential to look in the mirrors again and to consider a signal to deviate, if not previously given.

Horn: Should an audible warning be given? The driver must be guided by circumstances, bearing in mind that he could be in an area where the use of audible warning is prohibited.

Acceleration: Don't accelerate into a bend. The speed of the vehicle should be constant until you straighten up. The road conditions will also determine the rate of acceleration and where it should be applied.

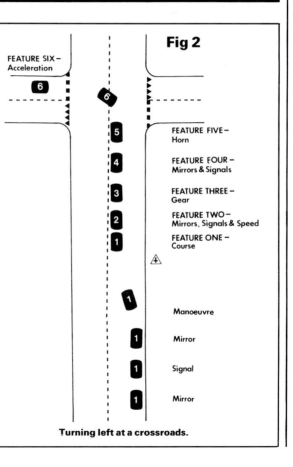

Fig 2

FEATURE SIX – Acceleration

FEATURE FIVE – Horn

FEATURE FOUR – Mirrors & Signals

FEATURE THREE – Gear

FEATURE TWO – Mirrors, Signals & Speed

FEATURE ONE – Course

Manoeuvre

Mirror

Signal

Mirror

Turning left at a crossroads.

Above right:

The driver having seen the hazard has used the mirrors to make sure it is safe to change course. A left turn direction signal has been given and speed is being reduced by braking. A gear change is not necessary as a Stop sign can be seen.

Right:

The mirrors have been used again, as the movement of any following traffic previously observed could have changed. Note the correct position of the vehicle on the road.

Above left:

The driver has brought the vehicle to rest at the correct position on the road; note the driver has kept off the area of white diagonal stripes. To enter this, except in an emergency, would be breaking the law.

Above:

The driver will get ready to move off and look left, right and left again. He must not move from this position until he is absolutely sure it is safe to do so.

Left:

The driver is in the correct position on the road to turn left. Each feature of the system was considered and if required used on the approach.

3 JUNCTIONS

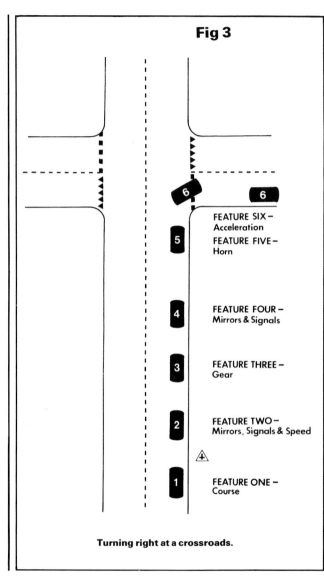

Fig 3

FEATURE SIX – Acceleration

FEATURE FIVE – Horn

FEATURE FOUR – Mirrors & Signals

FEATURE THREE – Gear

FEATURE TWO – Mirrors, Signals & Speed

FEATURE ONE – Course

Turning right at a crossroads.

Right:

The driver is on the ideal course being well to the right of the road, requiring little or no deviation from the normal safety position. The mirrors have been used and if circumstances require a change of position, a deviation signal should be considered before altering course.

Turning Right

Again, the procedure for turning right involves the simple use of the system of car control. See Figure 3.

1 Course: Unless there are any obstructions you won't have to change course to turn right. If there are obstructions and you have to signal to deviate past them, remember to look in the mirrors and remember too the possible confusion you could cause by indicating left if you intend to go right. The answer is not to move too far over to the right too early.

2 Mirrors, Signal and Speed: A direction indication may be required at this stage. Certainly you should be reducing speed having first checked in the mirror that it is safe to do so.

3 Gear: Select the correct gear for the turn.

4 Mirrors and Signal: If you haven't signalled your intention to turn right you should check in the mirror and do so now.

5 Horn: Is a pedestrian going to step out in front of you? Use of the horn in an unaggressive fashion may be necessary.

6 Acceleration: If it is safe to do so, the correct degree of acceleration should be applied to leave the hazard safely.

Far left, top:
The mirrors have been used again and a right turn directional signal given, a reduction of speed is being achieved by proper use of the brakes. A gear change is not necessary as a Stop sign can be seen.

Above left:
The driver has complied with the law and brought the vehicle to rest in the correct position on the road.

Left:
The driver has looked left, right and left again. He is absolutely sure it is safe to move off, which he is doing.

Roundabouts

A well known television advert would have you believe that European roundabouts are particularly dangerous. They aren't. They follow the same principles as those in the UK and it is hoped that this collection of photographs will put your mind at rest.

Right:
The general rule is to give way to traffic on the roundabout. Should it be otherwise, traffic signs/lights will inform the driver who has priority. Most roundabouts in the big towns and cities of Europe are controlled by light signals, therefore eliminating the problem of who has priority. This roundabout is in Reims, France.

Far left:
This roundabout in Berlin, Germany, has light signals as well. A driver must look well ahead and then the required information will be seen in good time.

Left:
Many roundabouts in the big cities of Europe have been engineered round a famous statue or monument. This one in Lisboa in Portugal, is a good example.

3 JUNCTIONS

Above right:

Traffic on a roundabout in Spain has the right of way, unless otherwise stated.

Right:

Traffic on a roundabout in Portugal has the right of way, unless otherwise stated by traffic signs.

4 Overtaking

Thoughtless overtaking at the wrong time and in the wrong place has been the cause of many fatal road accidents. You will have to pass many stationary and moving vehicles while abroad. To do so safely, you should apply the same system of car control that is used for fixed hazards. Of course, it is more complex because the 'hazard' is moving and because during the process of overtaking, a number of subsidiary hazards may arise and have to be dealt with in conjunction with the primary hazard.

Passing a stationary vehicle on the nearside of the road requires some thought, but presents little difficulty. The mirrors must be used well before applying Feature 1 (Course), and moving out to pass the obstruction. The driver then uses each feature of the system in sequence and as necessary. The horn (Feature 5) may need to be sounded if the stationary vehicle is occupied or there are signs of activity in or around it. On other occasions, where approaching traffic makes it unsafe to pass, the driver must vary his speed and gear or even stop altogether. A slow-moving vehicle (eg a heavy goods vehicle going uphill) could increase its speed, making planning more difficult and judgement more critical.

There are times and places when it would be pointless and irresponsible to attempt to overtake another vehicle, but some drivers do so with at times fatal results. You must remember one very important factor: if you're in a right-hand drive vehicle, your view of the road will be restricted. So you must question the need to overtake — is it worth it? What is to be gained by it?

Left:
To follow a tram at this distance is too close to overtake. There could be something — even another tram — coming. To overtake, it will be necessary to pull back and then pull out (after due use of mirrors) to see if the road is clear.

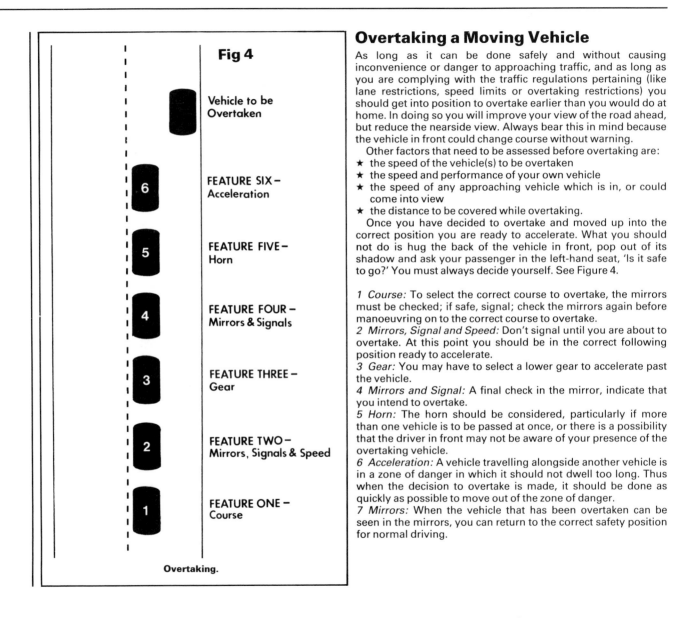

Fig 4

Vehicle to be
Overtaken

FEATURE SIX –
Acceleration

FEATURE FIVE –
Horn

FEATURE FOUR –
Mirrors & Signals

FEATURE THREE –
Gear

FEATURE TWO –
Mirrors, Signals & Speed

FEATURE ONE –
Course

Overtaking.

Overtaking a Moving Vehicle

As long as it can be done safely and without causing inconvenience or danger to approaching traffic, and as long as you are complying with the traffic regulations pertaining (like lane restrictions, speed limits or overtaking restrictions) you should get into position to overtake earlier than you would do at home. In doing so you will improve your view of the road ahead, but reduce the nearside view. Always bear this in mind because the vehicle in front could change course without warning.

Other factors that need to be assessed before overtaking are:
★ the speed of the vehicle(s) to be overtaken
★ the speed and performance of your own vehicle
★ the speed of any approaching vehicle which is in, or could come into view
★ the distance to be covered while overtaking.

Once you have decided to overtake and moved up into the correct position you are ready to accelerate. What you should not do is hug the back of the vehicle in front, pop out of its shadow and ask your passenger in the left-hand seat, 'Is it safe to go?' You must always decide yourself. See Figure 4.

1 Course: To select the correct course to overtake, the mirrors must be checked; if safe, signal; check the mirrors again before manoeuvring on to the correct course to overtake.
2 Mirrors, Signal and Speed: Don't signal until you are about to overtake. At this point you should be in the correct following position ready to accelerate.
3 Gear: You may have to select a lower gear to accelerate past the vehicle.
4 Mirrors and Signal: A final check in the mirror, indicate that you intend to overtake.
5 Horn: The horn should be considered, particularly if more than one vehicle is to be passed at once, or there is a possibility that the driver in front may not be aware of your presence of the overtaking vehicle.
6 Acceleration: A vehicle travelling alongside another vehicle is in a zone of danger in which it should not dwell too long. Thus when the decision to overtake is made, it should be done as quickly as possible to move out of the zone of danger.
7 Mirrors: When the vehicle that has been overtaken can be seen in the mirrors, you can return to the correct safety position for normal driving.

Far left, top:
There are places where overtaking is prohibited by law — thus the presence of white lines (road markings) and traffic signs. This traffic sign informs a driver that overtaking is prohibited.

Far left, bottom:
This is the sign that indicates the end of the overtaking restriction. The driver must bear in mind that it could still be unsafe to overtake due to other conditions.

Left:
There are no prohibitory overtaking signs or road markings present, but to overtake going down a steep gradient with an acute angled bend at the bottom would be very dangerous. This magnificent view is seen coming down the Grossglockner mountain in Austria.

4 OVERTAKING

Above right:
The white line must not be crossed, for the reason that can be seen emerging from the tunnel. A driver is not allowed to overtake while in the tunnel. To do so would be very dangerous apart from being illegal.

Far right, top:
The continuous white line prohibits a driver from overtaking. The view of the road cannot be seen to be clear, therefore the white line.

Right:
The continuous white line, combined with the illuminated overhead sign, informs you that you must stay in one lane.

Far left, top:
As can be seen by the traffic sign, there is a diversion ahead. It would be wise to hold back and let the lorry go first until the road ahead can be seen to be clear.

Above left:
The lorry in front is about to pull out to pass a stationary lorry. Hold back and wait for the situation to sort itself out, then re-evaluate the hazard before deciding whether or not to overtake.

Far left, bottom:
The nearside lane is for slow heavy goods vehicles, as can be seen by the broad broken white lines. Should a lorry be present in the nearside lane, a driver can overtake it by using the outside lane. In doing so the continuous white line must not be crossed.

Left:
Although it is permissible to overtake, it would be unwise to do so. Note the sharp bend that has a steep downhill gradient.

4 OVERTAKING

5 Mountains

One of the beauties of Europe — and also one of the drawbacks — is the breathtaking sight of high mountains. The Apennines, the Pyrenees and the Alps are so much bigger than anything visible in the UK. Driving over or through them is straightforward, but naturally you have to be on your guard. Changing weather conditions — especially in winter — can reduce visibility or even close a mountain pass and make driving difficult and treacherous. If you must travel through the mountains in winter — say for a skiing holiday — it is advisable to contact the tourist board of the country in question to clarify the routes and then take local advice on weather conditions rather than reaching the foot of a mountain to find the pass closed to traffic. If the pass is open, but snow is falling you must have snow chains and other aids available. In some countries it is a legal requirement to fit snow chains when the situation demands their use.

Another factor to be considered as well as the weather is the financial cost — particularly in tolls. If you are on a road that will require a toll to be paid it should be marked on a good 16 miles/24 miles to 1in scale map. Going round a mountain could be even more expensive!

Some vehicles are not suitable to negotiate a mountain either because the power-to-weight ratio is inadequate to climb a continuous gradient (some passes require a 1 in 5 climb!) or because of their width or length. On some passes the maximum permitted width is 7ft 6in and length is 30ft. Check your route carefully before travelling.

Finally remember one other factor. Older vehicles, particularly those that are well-laden, could well lose power at altitude. This will not cause problems if you are aware of the fact.

The following photographs show some of the things to be aware of in climbing and crossing mountain roads.

Right:
The information given by the sign states the name of the mountain (Grossglockner), that there is a toll, and the cost of the toll in Austrian and German currencies.

UMBRAILPASS

offen
ouvert / aperto
open

Zoll
20.00 – 0600
geschlossen / fermé
chiuso / closed

OFENPASS

offen
ouvert / aperto
open

Above left:

The driver is approaching the toll gate where the toll is paid. The red and green lights above the gates indicate which gate is open (green) and closed (red).

Above:

The information given by the sign is the name of the pass (Umbrailpass), that it is open and that there is a customs which is closed between the hours of 20.00 and 06.00, thus restricting the time that it can be used as a through road.

Left:

The sign tells the name of the pass (Ofenpass) and that it is open.

5 MOUNTAINS

Above:
The barrier would be closed if something had obscured the pass.

Far right, top:
Low cloud in the mountains can reduce visibility.

Right:
Same place, but look at the difference in conditions. This sort of change can occur very quickly in the mountains.

Left:

Positioning is of utmost importance before cornering and for road observation. Due to the acute angle of the numerous hairpin bends, the driver has positioned the vehicle well over to the right. Bear in mind that some mountain roads are unguarded, therefore a safety margin must be maintained at all times.

Below left:

Approaching the bend, the driver looks to the left to keep a careful look out for traffic ahead.

Below:

The sign gives the height of 2,571m — the summit.

5 MOUNTAINS

Descending a Mountain

Remember that primary braking must be by proper use of the brakes and not the gears. Remember too, that the distance you require to stop on a level, dry road is very different from that needed by a loaded car in the wet on a 1 in 5 gradient! Take it slowly; ensure you can always stop in the distance available. Keep a close eye on road conditions — gravel, cobblestones, tarmac, all affect tyre adhesion in different ways. It is silly to complain about slippery conditions *after* a skid.

Indeed, many road users are not as aware as they should be of the different road surfaces on which they drive. The majority of roads when dry are good or fairly good for roadholding. However, when the weather is wet the road surface becomes slippery: this is especially the case following a long spell of dry weather, when rubber dust and oil get washed to the road surface and cause tyres to lose adhesion. The presence of ice, frost, snow, mud and wet leaves have their own distinctive appearance, and must not be ignored, because they are factors that affect control of the vehicle.

When low cloud is present and in adverse weather, the headlights (with the beam dipped) must be switched on. For the purpose of photography in the next sequence of pictures, the vehicle is not using side or headlights, therefore making the point clearly.

Controlled, progressive braking is preferable to a sudden hard application of the brake. To maintain the stability of the car and equal distribution of weight while braking, the following rules should be applied.

1 Brake in good time, well before reaching the hazard, and thus give yourself time to select first gear for a hairpin bend.
2 Vary brake pressure to the road surface as skidding could occur if the road is wet.
3 Brake firmly on straight stretches and ease off just before the bend.
4 Engage a low gear at any early stage in the descent. This will assist control of speed by engine compression.

Left:
That's more like it. The full splendour of an alpine view.

Far left, top:

On leaving the summit of a mountain, a low gear should be engaged to assist control of speed with engine compression, thereby avoiding long periods of sustained braking.

Above left:

Check your brakes. It's a long way down. It is best to check the movement of handbrake and footbrake when you first enter the vehicle, and the footbrake again as soon as possible after moving off.

Far left, bottom:

The driver has applied the brake in good time, first gear has been selected and the clutch engaged. Effective observation to the right has been taken, in so doing approaching traffic will be seen in good time.

Left:

The driver is on the ideal course, requiring little or no deviation from the normal road position.

5 MOUNTAINS

Above right:

However sharp the bend, do not swing out before or after, as you will create a potentially dangerous situation for other road users who could be passing at the time.

The height of the mountain at this point is 2,583m. Note the unguarded road.

Right:

On a clear day, a driver can see the danger. Note the unguarded road that is in the direct line of travel. No driver can afford to make mistakes on roads like this.

Far left, top:

When fog or low cloud is present a driver will not always be aware of the danger. Don't be led into a false sense of security which is dangerous at any time, but particularly so when you're 2,500m up!

Above left:

The sheep can be seen in these weather conditions — but if it had been misty the danger would have been considerable to someone driving too fast.

Left:

The continuous white line in the middle of the road has the same meaning as in the United Kingdom; it should not be crossed. The warning sign informs a driver that there are road works ahead, therefore speed should be reduced so that the hazard can be seen in good time. This will give the driver time to take any appropriate action.

5 MOUNTAINS

Right:
By looking across a bend the driver will be able to see and assess the severity of the next bend.

Far left and above left:
The driver must give all his concentration to driving the vehicle and not to the scenic view. If you want to look at the scenery, park the car in a car park — as here (above). Do not stop on the road; it could be dangerous. The warning signs inform the driver that there is a steep descent for 6km. The road surface could be slippery and ice could be on the carriageway and heavy showers could occur.
Left:
Remember to ensure that you have enough fuel when you go into the mountains. While there are roadside telephones, should you get into difficulties, you shouldn't use them unnecessarily. The other sign shows that the road is an alpine postal route. On roads like these be particularly careful when passing buses or other PSVs.

5 MOUNTAINS

6 Motorways

VITESSE LIMITÉE EN FRANCE	SPEED LIMITS IN FRANCE
Sauf signalisation contraire	Unless otherwise indicated
60 En agglomèration	In built up areas
90 Sur route ordinaire	On normat roads
110 Sur route à deux chaussées séparées	On dual carriage ways
130 Sur autoroutes	On motorways
Port obligatoire de la ceinture de sécurité	Safety belt must be worn

Right:
Speed limits are clearly indicated together with the exhortation to wear a safety belt.

The motorways of Europe — autoroutes, autostrada, autobahnen — are similar to those of the UK and shouldn't cause concern to the first-time traveller in Europe. They are designed to make for a safer, faster ride and have reduced enormously the time necessary to make long journeys. But the laws — particularly those on speeding — are enforced rigorously.

Tolls on Motorways

The major difference between UK and European motorways is the levying of tolls — something to be borne in mind when costing out a holiday. The major credit cards are taken in some places — particularly in France and Spain. This can be helpful if you don't have local currencies available — or haven't enough money left!

When you approach a Toll area you stop to pick up a ticket from the Toll machine; this is handed in when you reach the Toll booth at the end of the Toll section when the fee is calculated and paid. The accompanying illustrations show this operation and other points about motorway driving.

Left:

Drivers join a motorway from a slip road that progresses into an acceleration lane. Note the warning sign (triangle) telling the driver that traffic on the motorway has priority.

Below left:

A driver on the slip road must give way to traffic on the motorway. Should a driver force his way into the traffic on the motorway, in doing so he will be committing an offence — even if a signal has been given. Remember, giving a signal simply tells the other road users what you want to do — it doesn't give you right of way.

When approaching the motorway always look in your mirrors and, if you can do so safely, look over your left shoulder to check the movement and position of any traffic on the motorway.

Left:

A heavy goods vehicle is about to join this Belgian motorway. A driver on the motorway would at this stage be looking in the mirrors and indicating his wish to move into the nearside lane.

Above right:

The view from the motorway. Should a change of course have to be made to overtake, then the mirrors must be used in good time before a change of course can be considered.

Right:

The sign on a German motorway reminds a driver to drive on the right, if it is safe to do so.

Far right:

There are times when a driver will have to change course. As can be seen by the traffic sign, the lane closure will force movement on to an outside lane.

Above left:
Toll ahead on a motorway in France.

Left:
Be brief — in English that means have the correct money available and don't hold up other road users.

6 MOTORWAYS

Right:

This is the machine that greets you at the toll booth. You can see that the tariffs are clearly indicated for both lorries (upper) and cars (lower). You simply press the button and take the ticket.

Far right, top:

On arriving at the toll office, the cashier will take the ticket. The cost of the toll to be paid will depend on how far you have travelled since collecting the ticket from the machine, and the class of vehicle used. The cashier has put the toll to be paid on the display panel, being 84 francs, which equals about £8. The motorway is A9 in France.

Far right, bottom:

Here on the French A7, the cost is greater than on the A9 as can be seen by the display sign. A saloon car is categorised as class one and the cost is 100 francs — about £10. You can see that travelling the length of France can be very expensive, more so if a return journey is made using the same motorway.

Above left:

Where there is considerable traffic movement at an interchange, or the interchange is complex, overhead gantry signs are used to direct traffic into the correct lane. As in the UK, these are well in advance of the interchange. This example is for East Germany.

Left:

Overhead gantry signals have a double pair of amber lights which flash and an illuminating symbol gives temporary maximum speeds or information about closed lanes. If the lights flash red, it means you should stop. The photograph was taken in Holland.

6 MOTORWAYS

Above right:
The message on this sign is obvious: the maximum speed for a vehicle towing a caravan is 80kph. Comply with the speed limits shown, because on-the-spot fines can spoil a holiday.

Right:
This sign shows that the speed restriction is over.

Far right:
This German sign informs a driver that there is a soft verge at the edge of the hard shoulder.

Far left, top:
There is a dangerous descent ahead on this French motorway. When you see a sign like this look in your mirrors immediately, you may have to apply your brakes.

Above left:
Emergency telephones are provided on both sides of motorways — the example is from France — sited in the verge at the back of the hard shoulder. They are identified by a number and the letters SOS.

Left:
Always pay attention to the weather conditions ahead of you — this will enable you to slow down in good time if there is need to. Remember that you must be able to stop your vehicle within the distance you can see to be clear.

6 MOTORWAYS

Above:
The sign on the right illuminates when an approaching vehicle is exceeding 60kph, as a warning to slow down.

Above right:
This sign illuminates when a vehicle approaches it, as a reminder to reduce speed before entering the bend.

Right:
Roadworks ahead! A change of course will have to be made. Use your mirrors so that you know where any following traffic is; you may have to reduce speed.

Above left:

As a last resort — an example of which is seen on this East German motorway — one side of the carriageway will have to be closed. In such an event, traffic from the other side of the motorway will have to be diverted through the gap in the central reservation to the opposite side of the carriageway; this is called 'contra-flow'. Every precaution should be taken when travelling in what has become a two-way traffic system.

Left:

If you decide to go to Berlin on the A2 from Hanover, you will pass through this checkpoint.

Above right:
A watchtower on the East German motorway en route to Berlin. The presence of these towers makes a driver aware of the speed limits at all times.

Far right, top:
There are excellent service areas on the motorways of Europe, especially the autobahns of West Germany, where the selection of refreshments is excellent. A driver going to Berlin is advised to stop and eat in a West German service area and not in an East German one. You will certainly notice the difference should you decide to do so. This sign on a French motorway shows services available.

Right:
A very basic service area on a Portuguese motorway — no refreshments, just petrol pumps and a toilet.

Above left:
Should it become necessary to overtake, the vehicle in front must be overtaken on the left. The car in front is overtaking a heavy goods vehicle, when he is in a safe position to do so the driver will return to the right-hand lane.

Left:
When intending to leave the motorway, you must position the vehicle in the right-hand lane in good time. If needed, a signal should be given in good time.

6 MOTORWAYS

7 General

Breakdowns

In the event of a breakdown or puncture you should get your vehicle off the road if you can. If you cannot, any passenger(s) should leave the vehicle and get clear of the road. You should then take appropriate action to warn other road users of an obstruction: if the vehicle is fitted with hazard warning lights they should be used. Should a breakdown occur during the hours of darkness, fog, mist, heavy rain or snow, the obligatory (side) lights should be left on together with hazard warning lights. The same procedure should apply in poor daytime visibility. A warning triangle should be placed on the road at least 50m from the vehicle and 150m on the hard shoulder of motorways. Should equipment have to be removed from the rear of the vehicle to assist in the repair of the breakdown, you should take care not to obscure the rear lamps from approaching traffic, thus defeating their object.

If anything falls from your vehicle stop as soon as safely possible. The appropriate hazard lights and side lights plus the warning triangle should be used and you should then remove from the carriageway whatever has fallen from the vehicle. This procedure is not allowed on a motorway.

Right:
A warning triangle placed in this position is illegal and irresponsible. The minimum distance required by law in most European countries is 50m from the hazard on the type of road shown. A warning triangle must not be used as an excuse for illegal parking or stopping.

Above left:
The warning triangle has been placed on the road at the correct distance, 50m from the hazard.

Left:
Should a breakdown occur just after a bend, the warning triangle should be placed on the road on the approach to the bend, as shown. On the approach to dead ground, the triangle should be placed on the approach to the crest so that it can be seen before the hazard is reached.

7 GENERAL

Tunnels

Right:

In good daylight and weather conditions, the oncoming hazard can be seen in good time. Note the lay-by on the right.

When in a tunnel it is an offence to:
- **Reverse.**
- **Turn round.**
- **Overtake another motor vehicle where there is only one lane going in the direction of travel.**
- **Stop. You can only do this in an emergency. If you have to stop turn off the engine (because of the danger of exhaust fumes). The breakdown signal (warning triangle) should be placed at least 50m from the vehicle, at the edge of the road so that it is clearly visible to other road users. Hazard warning lights can also be used when fog is present, for obvious reasons.**

When following another vehicle into a tunnel you must maintain a separation distance of 70m from the vehicle in front. The 70m is required by law in many countries.

Far right:

Compare this photograph with that on the left. Same place, vastly different weather conditions. The dangers are obvious: don't drive too fast for the prevailing conditions!

Far left, top:

Take off your sunglasses before you enter a tunnel so that your eyes have time to adapt to the different light. This applies whether a tunnel is lit or not.

Here a coach is about to leave the tunnel. There are no lights on, thus making it very difficult to see on entry.

There is a pedestrian footpath on the right of the road.

Above left:

When low cloud or fog is present, the entrance to a tunnel is obscured. Again emphasising the need for the use of headlights in tunnels.

Far left, bottom:

When leaving a tunnel, the traffic signs remind you to turn off your headlights (subject to the weather and lighting conditions at the time). The other sign shows the end of the previous maximum speed limit.

Note how the road weaves its way up the mountain.

Left:

This tunnel has a traffic light system in operation. Note also the recommended speed limit — 32kph; the name of the tunnel (Belchen) and its length. The tunnel is well lit but dipped headlights should still be used.

7 GENERAL

Right:

Two pedestrians have just left a Spanish tunnel which has a footpath.

Far right:

This photograph shows clearly why headlights (beam dipped) should be used. The footpath is very narrow with little or no kerb separating it from passing traffic. A driver's eyes take a few seconds to adjust to the different lighting conditions and it is during this time that pedestrians may not be seen.

Right:

Single-track tunnels are rare, but mean that traffic is controlled by signals that can be seen at the entrance. If the red signal is showing, a driver must get into the appropriate lane as shown by the sign on the right and wait for the green before proceeding.

The four traffic signs at the entrance inform a driver that there is a 2.5m width limit, a 3.60m height limit, maximum speed in the tunnel is 60kph and a vehicle with a dangerous load is prohibited.

Level Crossings

Wherever a driver travels in Europe he will in all probability encounter a level crossing of one type or another. The type of crossings used are similar to those in the UK and you should act as the Highway Code of the UK outlines.

Left:
This is an automatic half-barrier level crossing in Holland. When the train has passed, wait for the barriers to go up. Do not be impatient.

Above:

The level crossing can be seen; should the warning lights start flashing, the driver will have to slow down and be prepared to stop.

Above right:

The warning lights are flashing and the barriers are being lowered on this Austrian crossing.

Right:

When the train has passed and the barriers have gone up, you may proceed.

Above left:
The warning sign painted on this Italian road informs you that there is a level crossing ahead — the railway can be seen converging from the left.

Left:
This is a single-track railway line in Portugal, with an open level crossing. The driver must comply with the traffic sign. When he is sure it is safe to proceed, the driver should do so and get clear of the crossing quickly.

7 GENERAL

Broken Windscreen

The most common cause of broken windscreens is a stone or other object thrown up from the wheels of another vehicle — although it has also been known for a heavy goods vehicle, going up a steep hill with its engine under strain, to create a particular pitch or drone which has shattered a windscreen of a passing vehicle. A loud bang is normal if a windscreen shatters, which can be disorientating.

You should take precautions on roads where loose stones or grit are present, by reducing speed and increasing the distance between you and the vehicle in front. In the event of a windscreen shattering, treat it as an emergency. Generally, it is not advisable to punch a hole in the screen to gain vision, because this may cause injuries and aggravate the situation by allowing pieces of glass to enter the car. All that is necessary is for the driver to pull into the side of the road as soon as practicably possible, and to stop.

If it is necessary to continue to drive before the windscreen is replaced, the air vents should be covered and the bodywork protected. The screen should then be pushed outwards and as much glass removed as possible. The vehicle should be driven slowly with the windows closed; this will prevent a through draught and will assist in protecting the driver and passengers from glass splinters. If suitable eye protection is available it should be worn. Sunglasses must not be worn for eye protection during the hours of darkness.

Unlike the United Kingdom, there is no 24-hour mobile windscreen replacement service in the majority of countries in Europe. Should a windscreen shatter while abroad, there will be no alternative but to contact the nearest garage who supplies and services the make of vehicle being driven. In all probability the vehicle will have to be driven to the garage where the replacement will take place. It is advisable to take a rolled-up emergency windscreen which will be a compromise until a proper replacement can be made.

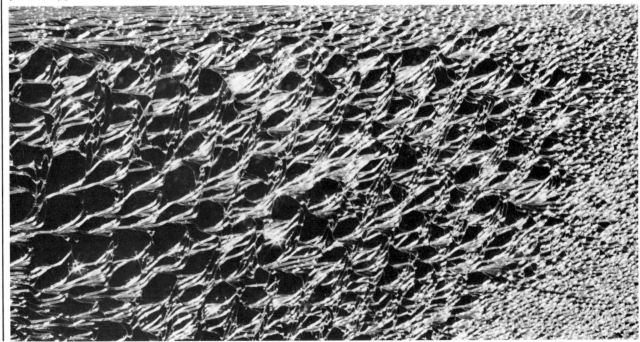

Right:
This is a driver's view of a toughened windscreen the moment it shatters. If travelling at speed it could collapse, creating thousands of fragments of glass which could be blown over the driver and front seat passenger. A laminated windscreen is safer than a toughened screen because it is less likely to shatter.

Stopping and Leaving Your Car

If you intend to park on the public highway you should first check in your mirrors that it is safe to do so. A signal by direction indicator should be considered to inform other road users and pedestrians of the intention to deviate or slow down. Speed should be reduced gradually, having due regard to traffic that can be following too closely.

Bring your vehicle to rest in a safe position close to the kerb or in a parking area or place provided. If you are aware of the contents of the Highway Code of the UK, you should have no problem in complying with the laws appertaining to motor vehicles, as they are similar in content in most countries of Europe. However, common sense must prevail. If you create or cause an obstruction, you will have to pay the penalty unless the circumstances are beyond your control, or to avoid an accident.

When you've stopped, your foot should remain on the brake pedal until the hand brake is applied and the gear lever/selector moved to neutral. If the vehicle is on a gradient, first gear should be selected if the vehicle is facing uphill and reverse gear selected for that of a downhill gradient, as an additional safety precaution. The engine and all unnecessary auxiliaries should then be switched off, and the seat belt stored neatly. For a vehicle with an automatic gearbox, the gear selector should be moved to the 'P' position.

Before leaving the vehicle unattended, the driver should carry out the following checks:
● Remove the ignition key and activate the steering lock.
● Close all windows.
● Put any valuables out of sight, preferably in the boot.
● Lock all doors, the boot and sun roof.

Make sure it is safe to get out of your vehicle before you do — bearing in mind that you are driving a right-hand drive vehicle in a left-hand drive country. Look over your right shoulder for pedestrians who could be passing. Any passenger(s) are advised to alight from the vehicle on the right (pavement side), thus preventing them getting involved with traffic that could be passing. This applies particularly to children, as they will in all probability be unaware of the danger, and open a door in the path of passing traffic.

Left:
Make sure you comply with the law before parking your vehicle. Before leaving the vehicle unattended, a driver should carry out the following checks:
● **Remove the ignition key and activate the steering lock.**
● **Close all windows.**
● **Put all valuables out of sight, preferably in the boot.**
● **Lock all doors, the boot and sunroof.**

Below:
Many times you will have to check your map to confirm the right route. If you have to, it is advisable to pull off the road where practicable so as not to obstruct other traffic.

Right:
A lay-by is an ideal place to pull up and rest; at the same time check the maps for your intended route.

Below:
The driver of this vehicle in Amsterdam did not comply with the conditions for parking at a meter. An official can be seen applying a wheel clamp.

Below right:
The wheel clamp is in position. The driver will have to pay the fine of about £40 before the clamp is removed.

Far left, top:
The traffic warden is waiting for the driver to return and move the vehicle. The driver did not return and a ticket was issued.
Location: Sevilla, Spain

Far left, bottom:
This German sign advises drivers that they are entering a No Parking zone. Apart from certain specific exceptions (hotel guests and shopping for 15min maximum, etc) the car park is indicated. Many villages and towns on the continent have narrow streets and parking restrictions.

Left:
A complicated sign with lots of foreign words on it. Ignorance of the law is no excuse — if you don't understand either ask a passer-by or move to a regular car park.

Right:
The driver of this vehicle did not comply with the traffic sign and his car is being taken away to a Police compound where he will have to go to pay the fine. This is the most expensive (in more ways than one) method of illegal parking.
Location: Wien (Vienna), Austria

Far left, top:
These parking meters in Zurich can be used for 30min. After that time an offence will have been committed.

Above left:
The information on this Italian traffic sign doesn't need translation. There are those who do push their luck.

Far left, bottom:
A woman with one young child in her arms and another at her side is attempting to cross the road. Cars have been parked in dangerous positions, and in so doing obscure a driver's view of the crossing as it is approached. This photograph shows how important observation is in driving abroad.

Left:
Cars have been parked either side of the crossing. This type of parking would never be allowed in the UK.

7 GENERAL

8 Only in Europe

Road Surfaces

Most of the roads in Europe have a surface of asphalt or other compounds which may have a dressing of stones or chips. These have a comparatively high non-skid value and are easily recognised. In time they take on a polished appearance and lose some of their non-skid properties. There are other types of road surface that become very slippery in wet weather, particularly during a shower of rain following a long spell of dry weather.

Right:
This type of road surface has a good non-skid value.

Above left:
Cobblestones and tramlines are encountered occasionally in towns and cities. Great care must be taken when driving on these surfaces to avoid skidding.

Left:
This is a good example of one of the most dangerous types of bend a driver will encounter, more so when the road is wet. The road surface is cobblestones, there is a downhill gradient and a right-hand bend. Should a driver approach this bend too fast or brake hard when the road surface is wet, control of the vehicle would be lost. Proper use of observation and acceleration sense will minimise the risk.

8 ONLY IN EUROPE

Customs

When leaving one country to enter another you will have to go through a customs control. If requested, you will have to show various documents and on occasion the vehicle and its contents will be checked. Provided the documents are in order, and nothing illegal is being transported, you should have no concern.

Right:
Entering Italy from Austria.

Above left:
Entering Austria from Liechtenstein.

Far left:
Entering Germany from Holland. The sign on the right, ZOLL, means that you must stop at the customs house, even if the customs authorities do not always stop and check the vehicles. You must also not exceed 20kph in the area of the customs post.

Left:
Entering Portugal from Spain.

8 ONLY IN EUROPE

Above right:

To enter East Berlin from the West you must go through Allied Checkpoint Charlie. The Western customs house can be seen in the middle of the road.

Far right, top:

Once through the checkpoint, a traveller will pass East German guards, here armed with guns and cameras. Not a welcome sight to any visitor! The Berlin Wall can be seen in the background.

Right:

Alfandega **is Portuguese for customs. The customs post is 200m away.**

Far right, bottom:

Leaving Portugal for Spain.

Trams and Trolleybuses

The majority of the largish cities in Europe have trams and/or trolleybuses as a means of public transport. It should always be borne in mind that the position in which these vehicles travel on the road varies from one country to another. It should also never be forgotten that a tram cannot change its position of direction of travel on the road to suit a particular traffic situation.

Left:
On the approach to a junction a positive effort must be made to look for the clues from which an accurate assessment of the hazard can be made. The road markings show that you must give way to traffic on the major road, and a tram is passing by. A driver who arrives at a junction at the same time as that of an approaching tram should wait until the tram has passed before emerging, even if he thinks there is adequate time and space to proceed. Note also that there is no left turn.

8 ONLY IN EUROPE

Above right:
Do not stop or park a vehicle where it will obstruct the passage of a tram — as it could do if parked on this Belgian road.

Right:
Lane markings can be clearly seen. The broad white line separates trams from other traffic, and should not be crossed.

Far right:
If a driver of a trolleybus indicates his intention to leave an official bus stop, by using the direction indicator, vehicles approaching from behind must, if necessary, slow down or stop to enable the bus driver to move off. When passing a stationary bus, watch out for passengers getting on or off. Give way to tram passengers who alight directly on to the road ahead of you. Stop until they have passed.
Location: Zurich, Switzerland

Above left:

Trams in Vienna (Wien), Austria, travel near the kerb; in so doing they reduce the possibility of injury to passengers who leave the footpath to board the tram or as they alight.

Left:

When trams occupy the nearside of the road, the potential danger to drivers arises when a right turn has to be made. In such a case the tramlines will have to be crossed, like traffic turning right in the photograph. The mirrors must be used, and any tram that can be seen following should be given precedence, unless traffic signals control the movement of traffic and trams. The Vienna Opera House can be seen in the background.

Above right:

In this road in Zurich, Switzerland, trams travel in each direction on one side of the road and traffic goes one way on the other half, thus eliminating the need to overtake them.

Right:

It is important to consider where a vehicle is brought to rest, especially where trams pass. Should a vehicle be parked on bends — like this one in Basel, Switzerland — a tram that is passing could collide with it, due to the overhang of the tram swinging out as it goes round the bend. Thus extensive damage could be the result of inconsiderate or thoughtless parking. As mentioned previously in this chapter, trams cannot change their position on the road to suit the ever-changing or prevailing traffic conditions.

Far left:

When the road is narrow and a tram is present, there is no option but to follow the tram — as is graphically illustrated in this photograph of Antwerp, Belgium. A tram ahead has stopped at a tram stop, passengers can be seen alighting; therefore a driver must be patient and wait at a safe distance (at least 2m), until it moves off. When it does, a safe distance must be maintained.

Above left:

As a rough guide, the width of the handlebar on the moped is approximately a third of the width of an average saloon car. It can be seen from this photograph of Basel that no attempt to overtake the tram should be made, as there will be no margin of safety should an unexpected situation arise — added to which the road ahead cannot be seen to be clear.

Left:

The tram is moving off from a tram stop as vehicles overtake it. The width of the road on the nearside is wide enough to be able to overtake a tram with a good margin of safety. At the same time, a driver must be aware of the stationary vehicles on the right which create a potential danger.

Location: Antwerpen, Belgium

8 ONLY IN EUROPE

Above right:

When a left turn has to be made, a driver must be absolutely sure there is no tram following, approaching or, as in this situation, that a tram moves off before he starts to turn. If in any doubt a driver should stop and assess the situation further. Another factor which must be considered is the presence of any pedestrian(s) before the decision to change course is made. This photograph shows the situation at the front of Bremen main station in West Germany.

Far right:

The road to nowhere. This was one of the roads that took a visitor to the centre of Berlin, but does no more. The Berlin Wall — constructed in 1961 — separates the East from the West.

Right:

There is no road along the wall, only a footpath.

Above left:

When a driver or passengers alight from a vehicle they become pedestrians and the passengers in particular have to take more note of the surrounding traffic. The crowded continental cities — here Basel is illustrated — with their trams can be daunting — but all you need to remember is the direction the traffic is moving and to take care as you cross the roads.

Left:

Before stepping off a footpath a pedestrian must check to see if the road is safe to cross by looking left, right and left again; if in any doubt, wait. Young children should be looked after at all times and never be allowed to wander off. A tram can be seen approaching, and once it has passed the road must be re-checked to see if any other traffic is approaching. Only when it is safe to do so, should the road be crossed. In some cities there are subways which provide a safe place to cross a road. This is another photograph of Basel, Switzerland.

Road Signs

Above right:
This French road sign tells drivers to keep a minimum distance of two car lengths between them in foggy conditions and at a maximum speed of 50kph/30mph.

Right:
The sign speaks for itself.

Far left, top:
This Spanish sign warns a driver that the maximum height of the approaching tunnel is 3.8m. A vehicle that is over 3.8m must use the lane on the right, which will take them round the tunnel.

Above left:
Note the speed limit of 50kph/30mph and the No Overtaking signs, the reasons why are clearly seen.

Far left, bottom:
This police officer has stopped the traffic to let a tram pass.

Left:
The pedestrians in Strasbourg are taking advantage of the signal given by the police officer.

8 ONLY IN EUROPE

Above:

On your return journey, you will see this sign in the town directing you to the ferry. On arriving at the harbour, the procedure will be the same as when you left the UK.

Above right:

Once you leave the ferry, you will have to go through passport control and then the customs.

Right:

The sign warns a driver that ice could be on the road. *Hielo* is Spanish for ice.

Far left:
In the majority of European countries, warning and traffic signals are given overhead as well as on the side of the road. These illuminated signs are a warning of danger, when the amber lights flash the mirrors must be used if necessary and speed must be reduced. Here in Liechtenstein this illuminated amber light warns a driver that there is a pedestrian crossing ahead.

Above left:
The amber lights are flashing, warning a driver that the traffic light signals that can be seen in the distance are at red. The mirrors should be used and speed reduced. This photograph was taken in Spain.

Left:
This speed limit sign informs a driver that the maximum speed limit in favourable conditions is 60kph.

8 ONLY IN EUROPE

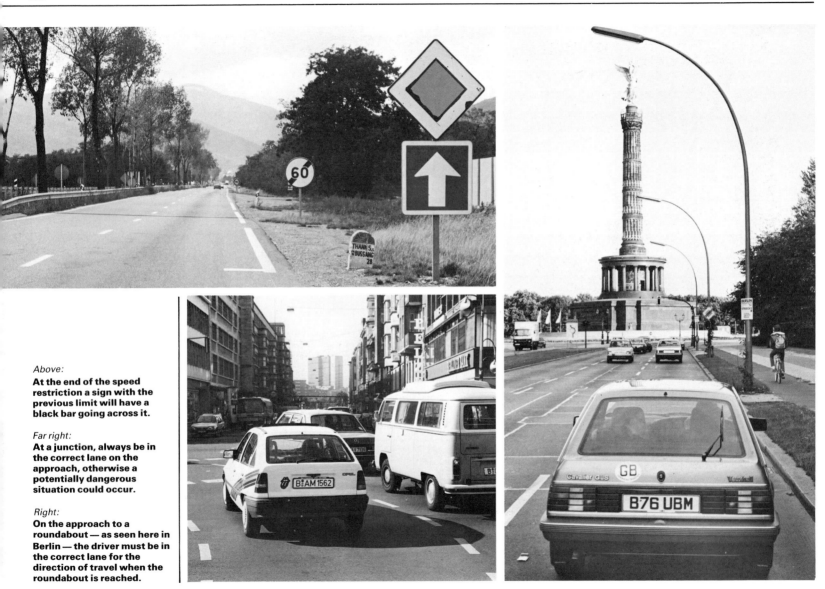

Above:
At the end of the speed restriction a sign with the previous limit will have a black bar going across it.

Far right:
At a junction, always be in the correct lane on the approach, otherwise a potentially dangerous situation could occur.

Right:
On the approach to a roundabout — as seen here in Berlin — the driver must be in the correct lane for the direction of travel when the roundabout is reached.

Far left:
This Berlin traffic light signal has one for cyclists and one for other traffic.

Left and below:
Whatever the traffic situation you must comply with traffic signs and stop at junctions, (left) shows a sign in Spain; (below) shows complicated Spanish lane markings.

8 ONLY IN EUROPE

Right:

Traffic signs may differ from those in the UK. Note that green and amber are on together before red is shown on this Italian sign.

Below:

When there is a strong wind, a cyclist could be blown on to the road, thus a safety margin must be maintained if possible.

Far right:

A driver should watch out for cyclists who could leave a cyclepath without looking.

Left:
Thank you and goodbye!

9 Useful Addresses

The following information will assist you to plan your journey. Legislation can change from one country to another, therefore if you think that further guidance is necessary, contact the appropriate tourist office.

Austrian National Tourist Office, 30 St George Street, London W1. Tel: 01-629-0461.

Belgian National Tourist Office, 38 Dover Street, London W1. Tel: 01-499-5379.

Danish Tourist Board, Sceptre House, 169 Regent Street, London W1. Tel: 01-734-2637.

Dutch National Tourist Office, 143 New Bond Street, London W1. Tel: 01-499-9367.

Finnish Tourist Board, 66 Haymarket, London SW1. Tel: 01-839-4048.

French Government Tourist Office, 178 Piccadilly, London W1. Tel: 01-491-7622.

German National Tourist Office, 61 Conduit Street, London W1. Tel: 01-734-2600.

Italian State Tourist Office, 1 Princes Street, London W1. Tel: 01-408-1254.

Luxembourg National Trade and Tourist Office, 36 Piccadilly, London W1. Tel: 01-434-2800.

Norwegian Tourist Board, 20 Pall Mall, London SW1. Tel: 01-839-6255.

Portuguese National Tourist Office, New Bond Street House, 1 New Bond Street, London W1. Tel: 01-493-3873.

Spanish National Tourist Office, 57 St James's Street, London SW1. Tel: 01-499-0901.

Swedish National Tourist Office, 3 Cork Street, London W1. Tel: 01-437-5816.

Swiss Tourist Office, Swiss Centre, 1 New Coventry Street, London W1. Tel: 01-734-1921.

The Caravan Club: East Grinstead House, East Grinstead, West Sussex RH10. Tel: 0342-26944.

The Camping and Caravan Club: 11 Lower Grosvenor Place, London SW1W OEY. Tel: 01-828-1012.

The National Caravan Council: Catherine House, Victoria Road, Aldershot, Hants GU11 1SS. Tel: 0252-318251.

Royal Yachting Association: Victoria Way, Woking, Surrey GU21 1EQ. Tel: 04862-5022.

The International Driving Permit: issued by the Automobile Association and Royal Automobile Club, for a statutory fee.

Foreign currency/travellers cheques: contact your Bank or Thomas Cook who will assist you.

Health: your local DHSS office can advise on health abroad, ask for forms SA30 and SA35. Form SA30 is supplied with AA 5 Star Service.